MASTERING
THE DISCOVERY
SALES MEETING

A Guide for
TECHNOLOGY SALES REPS

By

LYNN SHOURDS

MASTERING THE DISCOVERY SALES MEETING

A Guide for Technology Sales Rep

Copyright © 2024 By Lynn Shrouds

Printed in the United States of America

Why Should You Read This Book?

Why is this book essential for your growth in technology sales? My experience spans over 25 years in this dynamic field, encompassing a wide range of products and services from foundational hardware to cutting-edge software, SaaS, ERP, MSP, and the intricate domain of Cybersecurity. My focus has always been on sales training - a critical element in maintaining and enhancing your sales proficiency, much like regular exercise is essential for physical fitness.

This book is a comprehensive guide, distilling numerous discovery sales techniques that I have refined and validated throughout my career. It is an invaluable resource for new sales representatives starting from scratch, providing step-by-step guidance to master the art of the deal. Moreover, it offers experienced sales professionals the opportunity to discover new strategies and tactics that might have previously eluded them.

A significant portion of this book addresses advanced challenges such as handling objections and effectively closing deals. These are pivotal moments that define a sales representative's capability. I offer practical advice, drawn from real-life scenarios and proven techniques, to empower you to approach these challenges with both confidence and skill. This book aims to accelerate your journey to becoming an adept sales professional in the tech industry. I invite you to join me in exploring the intricate and rewarding world of technology sales. Whether you are looking to build foundational skills or to refine and expand your existing knowledge, this book is your comprehensive guide to Mastering The Discovery Sales Meeting.

CONTENTS

MASTERING
THE DISCOVERY
SALES MEETING

A Guide for
TECHNOLOGY SALES REPS

" Statistics suggest that when customers complain, business owners and managers ought to get excited about it. The complaining customer represents a huge opportunity for more business."

- ZIG ZIGLER

Introduction to the Discovery Sales Meeting

The Importance of the Discovery Sales Meeting

In the world of technology sales, the discovery sales meeting is an integral part of the sales process. It is during this meeting that a sales representative has the opportunity to uncover the needs, pain points, and goals of a potential customer. This chapter will delve into the importance of the discovery sales meeting and how it can be a game-changer for technology sales reps.

First and foremost, the discovery sales meeting allows the sales rep to gather crucial information about the customer's current situation. By asking strategic questions and actively listening to the responses, the rep can gain a deep understanding of the customer's pain points and challenges. Armed with this knowledge, the rep can position their technology solution as the perfect fit to address these pain points, thus increasing the chances of closing the deal.

Furthermore, the discovery sales meeting is an opportunity for the sales rep to build rapport and establish trust with the customer. By showing genuine interest in the customer's business and actively engaging in a conversation, the rep can create a connection that goes beyond the transactional nature of the sales process. This connection can lead to long-term customer relationships and repeat business.

Additionally, the discovery sales meeting allows the sales rep to differentiate themselves from the competition. By thoroughly understanding the customer's needs and pain points, the rep can tailor their pitch to highlight the unique benefits and features of their technology solution. This personalized approach sets the rep apart from competitors who may take a more generic approach to sales.

Moreover, the discovery sales meeting is an opportunity for the sales rep to educate the customer about the various features and capabilities of their technology solution. By effectively communicating the value proposition, the rep can showcase how the technology can solve specific problems and drive business growth. This education process is essential for the customer to make an informed purchasing decision.

The discovery sales meeting is a critical step in the technology sales process. It provides an opportunity for sales reps to gather vital information, build rapport, differentiate themselves from competitors, and educate the customer about their technology solution. By mastering the art of the discovery sales meeting, technology sales reps can significantly increase their chances of success and drive business growth.

Understanding the Role of Technology Sales Reps

The role of a sales representative is crucial in driving business growth and success. As a technology sales rep, your primary responsibility is to engage in discovery sales meetings, where you have the opportunity to showcase the value and benefits of your company's products or services. This chapter aims to provide you with a comprehensive understanding of your role in these meetings and equip you with the necessary skills to excel.

The discovery sales meeting is a pivotal moment in the sales process, where you get to connect with potential clients on a deeper level. It is during this meeting that you have the chance to understand their unique needs, pain points, and goals. Your role as a sales rep is to ask insightful questions, actively listen, and empathize with their challenges. By doing so, you can tailor your product or service offerings to meet their specific requirements effectively.

Reps must possess a deep understanding of their company's products or services. This knowledge will enable you to articulate the features, functionalities, and advantages of your offerings clearly. By showcasing how your technology solutions can solve their problems and enhance their business operations, you can position yourself as a trusted advisor and build credibility with potential clients.

Another critical aspect of your role as a technology sales rep is to stay up to date with the latest industry trends and advancements. Technology is constantly evolving, and it is essential to remain knowledgeable about emerging technologies and how they can benefit your customers. By staying informed, you can demonstrate your expertise and present innovative solutions that give your company a competitive edge.

Furthermore, effective communication skills are paramount. You must be able to communicate complex technical concepts in a clear and concise manner, ensuring that potential clients understand the value proposition of your offerings. Additionally, active listening skills are essential to truly understand the needs and concerns of your prospects, allowing you to tailor your sales pitch accordingly.

Your role in discovery sales meetings is vital to the success of your company. By understanding the unique needs of potential clients, effectively communicating the value of your offerings, staying informed about industry trends, and honing your communication skills, you can excel in your role and drive business growth. Mastering the art of the discovery sales meeting will not only benefit you as a sales rep but also contribute to the overall success of your organization.

Setting Goals for the Discovery Sales Meeting

This chapter aims to guide technology sales reps on how to set effective goals for their discovery sales meetings, ensuring that they maximize their chances of success.

The discovery sales meeting is an opportunity for sales reps to gather vital information about a potential client's needs, pain points, and objectives. It is a chance to dig deep into their business challenges and present tailored solutions that can address their specific requirements. However, without clear goals, these meetings can become unproductive and fail to yield the desired outcomes.

The first step in setting goals for a discovery sales meeting is to conduct thorough research on the potential client. This includes studying their industry, competitors, and any recent developments that might impact their business. This research will provide valuable insights that can help sales reps craft relevant and targeted questions during the meeting.

One important goal for a discovery sales meeting is to establish rapport and build trust with the client. This can be achieved by actively listening to their concerns, showing empathy, and demonstrating industry expertise. Building a strong rapport will create a foundation of trust, making it easier for the client to open up about their challenges and requirements.

Another goal is to uncover the client's pain points and needs. By asking thought-provoking questions, sales reps can delve deep into the client's business operations and identify areas where their solutions can make a significant impact. Understanding the client's pain points will allow sales reps to tailor their presentations and proposals to address these specific challenges.

Additionally, setting a goal to gather information about the client's decision-making process and timeline is crucial. This will help sales reps understand the client's expectations and align their strategies accordingly. It will also enable them to forecast the potential length of the sales cycle and allocate resources effectively.

By setting clear goals for their discovery sales meetings, technology sales reps can maximize their chances of success. These goals should focus on building rapport, uncovering pain points, and gathering essential information about the client's decision-making process. With effective goal-setting, sales reps can navigate discovery sales meetings with confidence and increase their chances of closing deals and building long-term partnerships.

If you aim at nothing, you will hit it every time."

- ZIG ZIGLER

Preparing for the Discovery Sales Meeting

Conducting Pre-Meeting Research

As a technology sales rep, one of the most crucial steps in preparing for a successful discovery sales meeting is conducting thorough pre-meeting research. This chapter will guide you through the process of gathering valuable information about your potential client, their industry, and their specific needs. By investing time and effort into this research, you can greatly improve your chances of delivering a tailored and effective sales pitch.

The first step in conducting pre-meeting research is to gather information about the company you will be meeting with. This includes understanding their industry, their competitors, their market position, and any recent news or developments that may impact their business. By having a comprehensive understanding of their company, you can demonstrate your knowledge and expertise during the meeting, which will help build trust and credibility.

Next, it is essential to research the key decision-makers you will be meeting with. This includes understanding their roles, responsibilities, and any previous interactions they may have had with your company. By knowing their background and interests, you can personalize your sales pitch accordingly, making it more relevant and compelling to their specific needs.

Additionally, conducting pre-meeting research should involve understanding the specific challenges and pain points your potential client is facing. By researching their industry trends, market demands, and potential obstacles, you can position your product or service as a solution to their problems. This will make your sales pitch more persuasive and demonstrate that you have taken the time to understand their unique needs.

Furthermore, gathering information about any existing solutions or competitors in the market is crucial. By understanding what your potential client is currently using or considering, you can highlight the advantages and differentiation of your product or service. This will enable you to position yourself as a superior option and address any concerns they may have about switching providers.

Conducting pre-meeting research is an essential step in mastering the discovery sales meeting as a technology sales rep. By investing time and effort into gathering information about your potential client, their industry, and their specific needs, you can deliver a tailored and effective sales pitch. This research will enable you to demonstrate your knowledge and expertise, build trust and credibility, and position your product or service as the ideal solution. Remember, preparation is key to success in the discovery sales meeting, and thorough pre-meeting research is a crucial part of that preparation process.

Creating an Agenda for the Discovery Sales Meeting

To make the most of your meeting, it is essential to have a well-structured agenda in place. In this chapter, we will explore the key elements that should be included in your agenda for a successful discovery sales meeting.

1. Introduction and icebreaker: Begin the meeting by introducing yourself and your company. Make a personal connection with the prospect by starting with a brief icebreaker. This will help establish rapport and set a positive tone for the rest of the meeting.

2. Objectives and expectations: Clearly state the objectives of the meeting and what you hope to achieve. Ask the prospect about their expectations and what they would like to get out of the meeting. This will ensure alignment and help you tailor the conversation accordingly.

3. Background research recap: Briefly summarize the research you have conducted on the prospect's company and industry. This demonstrates your preparedness and shows the prospect that you are genuinely interested in their business.

4. Needs assessment: This is the heart of the discovery sales meeting. Ask open-ended questions to encourage the prospect to share their pain points, challenges, and goals. Listen actively and take detailed notes to gain a comprehensive understanding of their needs.

5. Solution positioning: Once you have a clear understanding of the prospect's needs, it's time to position your product or

service as the solution. Highlight the features and benefits that align with their specific challenges. Use case studies or success stories to illustrate how your solution has helped similar organizations in the past.

6. Next steps and closing: Summarize the key points discussed during the meeting and confirm the prospect's interest in moving forward. Agree on the next steps, whether it's scheduling a follow-up meeting, providing additional information, or arranging a product demonstration.

7. Q&A and objections handling: Allocate time for the prospect to ask any questions they may have. Be prepared to address objections and concerns effectively. This is an opportunity to demonstrate your expertise and build trust with the prospect.

Remember, a well-structured agenda is just the starting point. Adapt it to the specific needs and preferences of your prospect. Be flexible and responsive throughout the meeting, allowing the conversation to flow naturally while keeping the agenda as a guide. By creating an agenda that covers all the essential elements, you can ensure a productive and successful discovery sales meeting.

Gathering Necessary Materials and Resources

This chapter, titled "Gathering Necessary Materials and Resources," aims to guide technology sales reps in preparing for these meetings effectively. By ensuring you have the right materials and resources at hand, you can maximize your chances of a successful outcome.

The discovery sales meeting is a vital step in the sales process, where you have the opportunity to understand your prospect's needs, challenges, and goals. To make the most of this valuable time, it is essential to gather the necessary materials and resources beforehand.

To reiterate, make sure you have a well-prepared agenda for the meeting. This will help you stay focused and ensure that all the important topics are covered. Include a brief introduction, objectives of the meeting, and a clear outline of discussion points. Having a structured agenda will show your professionalism and help you guide the conversation in the right direction.

Next, gather all relevant information about the prospect and their company. Research their industry, competitors, and latest news. This will not only demonstrate your commitment but also enable you to ask targeted and insightful questions during the meeting. Additionally, compile any previous communication records, such as emails or phone call notes, to ensure you have a comprehensive understanding of the prospect's previous interactions with your company.

In terms of resources, bring along product brochures, case studies, and any other relevant collateral that showcases your company's capabilities and success stories. These materials will serve as tangible evidence of your expertise and lend credibility to your claims. Additionally, consider bringing a laptop or tablet with a presentation prepared, highlighting key points and visuals that support your pitch.

Lastly, don't forget to bring a notepad and pen to take detailed notes during the meeting. Active listening and note-taking will not only help you remember important details but also show your prospect that you value their input. Jot down any specific pain points or requirements expressed by the prospect to refer back to later.

By gathering the necessary materials and resources, you will be well-prepared to lead a productive and engaging discovery sales meeting.

Remember, the more you invest in thorough preparation, the greater your chances of building trust, understanding your prospect's needs, and ultimately closing the deal.

" For every sale you miss because you're too enthusiastic, you will miss a hundred because you're not enthusiastic enough."

- ZIG ZIGLER

03

Building Rapport and Establishing Trust

The Power of First Impressions

In the world of technology sales, first impressions can make or break a deal. As a technology sales rep, you have the unique opportunity to establish a strong connection with potential clients during the discovery sales meeting. This chapter explores the powler of first impressions and provides valuable insights on how to make the most of this crucial moment.

The discovery sales meeting is the initial interaction between you and the client, where you have the chance to introduce your company, understand the client's needs, and build a foundation of trust. It is during this meeting that the client forms their first impression of you and your organization. Research has shown that first impressions are formed within seconds and can have a lasting impact on the outcome of the sales process.

To create a positive first impression, it is essential to be prepared and professional. Dress appropriately, arrive on time, and have all the necessary materials ready. Make sure you have done your homework and have a good understanding of the client's industry, challenges, and competition. This knowledge will help you showcase your expertise and build credibility from the start.

Non-verbal communication also plays a crucial role in first impressions. Maintain eye contact, smile genuinely, and use open and confident body language to convey trustworthiness and enthusiasm. Listen actively and show genuine interest in the client's needs and goals. By demonstrating empathy and understanding, you can establish a strong rapport and make the client feel valued.

Another key aspect of creating a positive first impression is the quality of your communication. Use clear, concise, and persuasive language to convey your message. Avoid jargon and technical terms that might confuse or alienate the client. Tailor your communication style to match the client's preferences, whether they prefer a more formal or informal approach.

Furthermore, it is crucial to showcase your value proposition early on. Clearly articulate how your technology solutions can address the client's pain points and deliver tangible benefits. Use compelling stories and case studies to illustrate how your products or services have helped other organizations achieve success.

Remember, first impressions are not only about what you say but also how you say it. Confidence, authenticity, and a genuine desire to help the client will leave a lasting positive impression. By mastering the art of making a powerful first impression, you can set the stage for a successful discovery sales meeting and lay the foundation for a fruitful long-term relationship with your clients.

Effective Communication Techniques

Mastering the art of effective communication is crucial for success. A successful discovery sales meeting requires not only a deep understanding of the product or service you are selling, but also the ability to effectively communicate that knowledge to your potential clients.

This chapter will provide you with valuable insights and techniques to enhance your communication skills and maximize your chances of closing deals during discovery sales meetings.

One of the most important aspects of effective communication is active listening. As a technology sales rep, it is imperative to listen attentively to your clients' needs, concerns, and objectives. By truly understanding their pain points and requirements, you can tailor your pitch to meet their specific needs, making it more likely for them to see the value in your offering.

Another essential communication technique is the art of asking powerful questions. By asking open-ended questions, you can encourage your clients to share more information about their challenges and goals. These questions should be thought-provoking and designed to stimulate a deeper conversation. By doing so, you not only gain valuable insights but also demonstrate your expertise and commitment to understanding your clients' needs.

Furthermore, effective communication involves the ability to explain complex concepts in simple terms. As a technology sales rep, you must be able to break down technical jargon and explain how your product or service can solve your clients' problems in a clear and concise manner. Avoid overwhelming your audience with too much information and focus on highlighting the most relevant benefits that align with their specific needs.

In addition to verbal communication skills, nonverbal communication also plays a vital role in your success as a technology sales rep. Pay attention to your body language, facial expressions, and tone of voice during discovery sales meetings. Maintain an open and approachable posture, make eye contact, and use a confident yet friendly tone to establish trust and rapport with your clients.

Lastly, effective communication also requires the ability to adapt your style to your audience. Not all clients have the same communication preferences, so it is essential to be flexible in your approach. Some clients may prefer a more formal and structured conversation, while others may appreciate a more friendly and casual approach. By adapting your communication style to each client, you can establish a stronger connection and improve your chances of closing the deal.

Mastering effective communication techniques is a crucial skill for technology sales reps during discovery sales meetings. By actively listening, asking powerful questions, simplifying complex concepts, paying attention to non-verbal communication, and adapting to your audience, you can enhance your communication skills and increase your chances of success in the competitive technology sales industry.

Active Listening Skills

Mastering the art of active listening is crucial for success in discovery sales meetings. As a technology sales rep, your ability to truly understand your clients' needs and pain points is what sets you apart from the competition. This chapter will delve into the importance of active listening skills and provide practical techniques to enhance your listening abilities during discovery sales meetings.

Active listening is more than just hearing what your clients are saying; it involves fully engaging with them and comprehending the underlying messages they are trying to convey. By actively listening, you demonstrate empathy, build trust, and develop meaningful relationships with your clients. This not only helps you gain a thorough understanding of their challenges but also allows you to tailor your solutions to meet their specific needs.

One of the most effective techniques for active listening is to maintain focused attention on the speaker. This means eliminating distractions, such as checking emails or thinking about what you'll say next, and giving your undivided attention to the client. By doing so, you can pick up on verbal and nonverbal cues that provide valuable insights into their thoughts and feelings.

Another important aspect of active listening is asking open-ended questions. These questions encourage clients to expand on their thoughts and provide you with a deeper understanding of their needs. By asking questions like "Can you tell me more about that?" or "How does this challenge impact your business?", you invite clients to share important information that can guide your sales approach.

Paraphrasing and summarizing what clients have said is another effective active listening technique. By restating their words in your own language, you demonstrate that you are actively engaged and have understood their message. This also gives clients the opportunity to clarify any misunderstandings or provide additional information.

Furthermore, active listening involves being mindful of nonverbal communication. Pay attention to clients' body language, facial expressions, and tone of voice to gain insights into their emotions and attitudes. Understanding these nonverbal cues can help you adapt your approach and better address their concerns.

In conclusion, active listening is an essential skill for technology sales reps during discovery sales meetings. By honing your active listening abilities, you can gain a deeper understanding of clients' needs, build stronger relationships, and offer tailored solutions. Implement the techniques discussed in this subchapter, and you'll be on your way to mastering the art of active listening in your technology sales career.

Building Trust with Prospects

Building trust with prospects is essential for success. The discovery sales meeting is a crucial opportunity to establish that trust, as it is the first real interaction between the sales representative and the potential customer. This chapter aims to guide technology sales reps on how to effectively build trust during the discovery sales meeting.

First and foremost, it is crucial to demonstrate expertise and knowledge about the product or service being offered. Prospects need to feel confident that the sales rep understands their unique challenges and can provide valuable solutions. Taking the time to thoroughly research the prospect's industry, competitors, and pain points will help the sales rep present themselves as a knowledgeable and credible resource.

Active listening is another key component in building trust. Sales reps should focus on understanding the prospect's needs and concerns, rather than solely pushing their own agenda. By actively listening and asking thoughtful questions, sales reps can demonstrate empathy and genuine interest in helping the prospect find the best solution for their business.

Transparency and honesty are vital when building trust. Sales reps should avoid making exaggerated claims or overpromising results.

Instead, they should provide realistic expectations and openly address any limitations or challenges associated with the product or service. This level of transparency will show prospects that the sales rep values their trust and is committed to building a long-term partnership.

Additionally, leveraging social proof can significantly enhance trust-building efforts. Sharing success stories, customer testimonials, or case studies that highlight how the product or service has helped similar businesses can instill confidence in prospects. It demonstrates that the solution has been proven and can deliver tangible results.

Finally, maintaining consistent and reliable communication throughout the sales process is crucial. This includes promptly responding to inquiries and providing updates on progress. By demonstrating reliability and professionalism, sales reps can further solidify trust with prospects.

In conclusion, building trust with prospects is a fundamental aspect of the discovery sales meeting. By showcasing expertise, actively listening, being transparent, leveraging social proof, and maintaining consistent communication, technology sales reps can establish a strong foundation of trust. This trust will not only increase the likelihood of closing deals but also pave the way for long-term customer relationships built on mutual respect and collaboration.

" Every choice you make has an end result."

- ZIG ZIGLER

04

Asking the Right Questions

Understanding the Types of Questions

The discovery sales meeting is where sales reps have the opportunity to gather important information about a potential customer's needs, pain points, and goals.

One of the key skills that every technology sales rep must master is the art of asking the right questions. The types of questions you ask during a discovery sales meeting can make or break your chances of closing a deal. That's why it's crucial to understand the different types of questions and when to use them.

1. Open-ended questions: These are questions that require more than a simple "yes" or "no" answer. Open-ended questions are designed to encourage the customer to provide detailed information. They often start with words like "what," "how," or

"why." For example, "What are your current challenges with your current technology solution?"

2. Closed-ended questions: These questions can be answered with a simple "yes" or "no" or a short response. Closed-ended questions are useful for clarifying specific details or confirming information. For example, "Do you currently have a budget for upgrading your technology?"

3. Probing questions: Probing questions go deeper into a customer's response to gain a better understanding. They help uncover additional information and can be used to explore pain points or challenges. For example, "Can you give me an example of how your current technology solution has hindered your productivity?"

4. Hypothetical questions: These questions are useful for exploring possibilities and potential future scenarios. They can help the customer envision how a new technology solution could benefit their business. For example, "If you were able to increase your efficiency by 20%, how would that impact your bottom line?"

5. Leading questions: Leading questions are designed to influence the customer's response. They can be used to guide the conversation towards a particular topic or highlight the benefits of a specific solution. However, it's essential to use leading questions ethically and avoid being manipulative.

Understanding the different types of questions and when to use them is a crucial skill for sales reps. By asking the right questions, you can gain valuable insights into the customer's needs and pain points, build trust, and position yourself as a trusted advisor. Remember to listen actively and adapt your questioning style based on the customer's responses. With practice, you'll become a master of asking questions that lead to successful discovery sales meetings and ultimately close deals.

In the realm of technology sales, the discovery sales meeting holds immense significance. This crucial stage of the sales process allows reps to gather valuable insights about their potential customers, understand their needs, and tailor their sales pitch accordingly. One of the most effective ways to extract this crucial information is through the art of questioning. However, not all questions are created equal.

Open-ended vs. Closed-ended Questions

In this chapter, we will explore the difference between open-ended and closed-ended questions and their respective applications in a discovery sales meeting.

Open-ended questions are designed to encourage the customer to provide detailed and thoughtful responses. These questions cannot be answered with a simple "yes" or "no" and instead require the customer to provide additional information, insights, or opinions. For example, "Can you tell me about your current technology infrastructure and the challenges you face?" or "What are your main goals and objectives for implementing a new solution?" These questions provide sales reps with a wealth of information, allowing them to uncover pain points, understand the customer's perspective, and build a stronger rapport.

On the other hand, closed-ended questions are concise and can be answered with a simple "yes" or "no" or a specific piece of information. While closed-ended questions may seem less valuable in a discovery sales meeting, they have their own significant role. These questions are ideal for gathering specific details or confirming information. For instance, "Is your budget for this project $50,000?" or "Are you the decision-maker for this purchase?" Closed-ended questions are effective in qualifying leads, ensuring that sales reps are targeting the right individuals and not wasting time on unqualified prospects.

The key to a successful discovery sales meeting lies in striking the right balance between open-ended and closed-ended questions. Open-ended questions help uncover challenges, aspirations, and motivations, while closed-ended questions provide the necessary clarity and specificity. By utilizing both types of questions strategically, technology sales reps can gain a comprehensive understanding of their potential customers and tailor their solutions to meet their unique needs.

Remember, the discovery sales meeting is not just about selling; it's about building relationships and establishing trust. By asking the right mix of open-ended and closed-ended questions, reps can demonstrate their expertise, empathize with the customer's challenges, and position themselves as trusted advisors rather than mere salespeople.

Using Probing Questions to Uncover Needs

The discovery sales meeting is when sales reps have the opportunity to uncover the needs of their potential customers and present tailored solutions that meet those needs. One powerful technique that sales reps can utilize during this meeting is the use of probing questions.

Probing questions are designed to dig deeper and extract valuable information from the customer. They are open-ended questions that encourage the customer to provide detailed responses, allowing the sales rep to gain a deeper understanding of their pain points and challenges. These questions enable the sales rep to uncover the true needs of the customer, which in turn helps them position their products or services effectively.

When using probing questions, it is important for technology sales reps to adopt a consultative approach. They need to act as trusted advisors rather than pushy salespeople. By asking thoughtful and strategic probing questions, sales reps can demonstrate their expertise and build rapport with the customer.

To effectively use probing questions, sales reps must prepare ahead of time. They should thoroughly research the prospect and their industry to gain a solid understanding of their pain points. This knowledge will enable them to ask relevant and targeted probing questions during the discovery sales meeting.

During the meeting, sales reps should start by asking general open-ended questions to gather basic information about the customer's business. As the conversation progresses, they can then delve deeper and ask more specific probing questions to uncover the underlying needs and challenges.

Some examples of probing questions that technology sales reps can use include:

1. "Can you tell me more about your current technology infrastructure and how it supports your business operations?"

2. "What are the key challenges you are currently facing in your industry, and how do you think technology can help address those challenges?"

3. "What specific goals or objectives do you hope to achieve by implementing new technology solutions?"

By asking these probing questions, sales reps can uncover valuable insights about the customer's pain points, business goals, and desired outcomes. Armed with this information, they can then present targeted solutions that address the customer's specific needs.

In conclusion, mastering the art of using probing questions during a discovery sales meeting is essential for technology sales reps. By adopting a consultative approach and asking thoughtful probing questions, sales reps can uncover the true needs of their customers and position their products or services effectively. This technique not only builds rapport with the customer but also increases the chances of a successful sale.

Avoiding Common Questioning Mistakes

The discovery sales meeting holds immense importance. This is the time when you, as a technology sales rep, have the opportunity to uncover your prospect's needs, pain points, and ultimately present your solution as the ideal fit. However, many sales reps make common questioning mistakes that can hinder their success in these crucial meetings. To help you avoid these pitfalls and maximize your chances of success, this subchapter will delve into the art of questioning in the discovery sales meeting.

One common mistake that sales reps often make is bombarding prospects with too many questions right from the start. While it is important to gather information, overwhelming the prospect with an excessive number of questions can make them feel interrogated and defensive. Instead, focus on building rapport and establishing a comfortable environment before delving into the questions. Start with open-ended questions that encourage the prospect to provide detailed responses and actively listen to their answers. This will not only make the conversation more engaging but also help you gain valuable insights into their pain points.

Another mistake to avoid is asking leading questions that steer the prospect towards a predetermined answer. This can undermine the authenticity of the conversation and make the prospect feel manipulated. Instead, aim for neutral, unbiased questions that allow the prospect to express their genuine thoughts and opinions. This will foster trust and credibility, enabling you to better understand their needs.

Furthermore, be mindful of the timing and flow of your questions. Rapid-fire questioning can create a sense of pressure and leave the prospect feeling overwhelmed. Give them ample time to respond and avoid interrupting their train of thought. Additionally, pay attention to their non-verbal cues and body language, as they can provide valuable insights into their level of engagement or discomfort.

Lastly, always be prepared with follow-up questions. While it is important to have a set of planned questions, adaptability is key. Tailor your follow-ups based on the prospect's responses to dig deeper into their pain points, challenges, and desired outcomes. This will demonstrate your attentiveness and genuine interest in their unique needs.

By avoiding these common questioning mistakes, you can enhance your discovery sales meetings, strengthen your relationships with prospects, and increase your chances of closing deals. Remember, the discovery sales meeting is not about a mere sales pitch; it's about understanding your prospect's world and positioning yourself as a trusted advisor.

" Your attitude, not your aptitude, will determine your altitude."

- ZIG ZIGLER

05

Identifying Customer Pain Points

Recognizing and Addressing Customer Challenges

During the discovery sales meeting, reps have the opportunity to uncover customer challenges and needs, laying the foundation for a successful sales process. Recognizing and addressing these challenges effectively is what sets top-performing technology sales reps apart from the rest.

One of the key aspects of recognizing customer challenges is active listening. Sales reps must listen attentively to the customer's pain points, concerns, and goals. By doing so, they can gain a deep understanding of the customer's needs and challenges. This active listening allows sales reps to tailor their solutions and demonstrate empathy, which builds trust and strengthens the customer-sales rep relationship.

Addressing customer challenges requires a proactive approach. Technology sales reps should be well-versed in the industry trends, market demands, and potential obstacles that their customers may face. By staying informed, sales reps can anticipate customer challenges and come prepared with innovative solutions. This proactive mindset showcases the sales rep's expertise and positions them as a trusted advisor rather than just another vendor.

Furthermore, sales reps must be skilled at asking the right questions. Effective questioning techniques help sales reps uncover hidden challenges and needs that customers may not initially be aware of. By delving deeper into the customer's pain points, sales reps can offer tailored solutions that address these challenges head-on. This approach not only demonstrates the sales rep's commitment to solving the customer's problems but also differentiates them from competitors who may take a more generic approach.

Once customer challenges have been identified, it is crucial to address them promptly and effectively. Sales reps should present their solutions in a clear and concise manner, highlighting how their products or services directly address the customer's specific challenges. Additionally, sales reps should be prepared to handle objections and provide evidence or case studies that validate their proposed solutions.

Recognizing and addressing customer challenges is a fundamental aspect of the discovery sales meeting for technology sales reps. By actively listening, staying informed, asking the right questions, and presenting tailored solutions, sales reps can position themselves as trusted advisors and increase their chances of closing deals successfully. Mastering this critical process will empower technology sales reps to navigate the complex world of customer challenges with confidence and proficiency.

Uncovering Hidden Pain Points

Uncovering hidden pain points are the key to understanding a prospect's needs, offering tailor-made solutions, and ultimately closing the deal. In this chapter, we will explore effective strategies to uncover these hidden pain points and maximize your chances of a successful sales meeting.

One of the first steps in uncovering hidden pain points is active listening. It is important to be fully present and engaged during the discovery meeting. Pay attention to not only what your potential client is saying, but also how they are saying it. Look for verbal and non-verbal cues that may indicate areas of concern or frustration. By actively listening, you can identify the pain points that are driving their decision-making process.

Another effective strategy is to ask probing questions. Don't be afraid to dig deeper and challenge assumptions. By asking open-ended questions, you can encourage your potential clients to share more about their pain points and the challenges they are facing. For example, instead of asking, "Do you have any issues with your current system?" try asking, "Tell me about the biggest challenges you face when it comes to your current system." This approach encourages a more detailed and honest response.

Additionally, conducting thorough research prior to the discovery sales meeting can provide valuable insights into the potential pain points your clients may be experiencing. Understanding their industry, competitors, and current technological landscape will enable you to ask more relevant and targeted questions. This will demonstrate your expertise and help build trust with your potential clients.

Finally, don't shy away from discussing past failures or mistakes. Sharing relevant examples of how you have helped other clients overcome similar pain points can be a powerful tool. It shows that you understand their challenges and have the experience and knowledge to solve them.

Uncovering hidden pain points is a critical step in the discovery sales meeting process. Active listening, asking probing questions, conducting thorough research, and sharing relevant examples are all effective strategies to maximize your chances of success. By understanding your potential clients' pain points, you can offer tailored solutions that address their specific needs, ultimately leading to a successful sales outcome.

Demonstrating Empathy and Understanding

The ability to connect with potential clients and truly understand their needs is crucial for success. This chapter explores the importance of empathy and understanding in the context of a discovery sales meeting, providing valuable insights and techniques for technology sales reps to master this essential skill.

Empathy is the ability to understand and share the feelings of another person. In a discovery sales meeting, demonstrating empathy towards your potential clients can significantly enhance your chances of building a strong rapport and establishing trust. By putting yourself in their shoes, you can better understand their pain points, challenges, and aspirations. This understanding will enable you to tailor your solutions and offerings in a way that resonates with their unique needs.

Understanding, on the other hand, goes beyond empathy. It involves actively listening, asking relevant questions, and gaining a deep comprehension of the client's business, industry, and objectives. By investing time and effort into understanding their specific circumstances, you can position yourself as a trusted advisor rather than just another salesperson. This approach will not only help you to identify the right solutions but also build a long-lasting relationship with the client.

To demonstrate empathy and understanding effectively, it is crucial to adopt a client-centric mindset. This means shifting your focus from your products or services to the client's needs and goals. By actively engaging in meaningful conversations and asking open-ended questions, you can uncover valuable insights that will guide your sales strategy and enable you to offer tailored solutions.

Active listening is another key component of demonstrating empathy and understanding. By giving your full attention to the client, maintaining eye contact, and providing verbal and non-verbal cues that indicate your interest, you show them that you genuinely care about their concerns. This level of attentiveness will not only make the client feel valued and heard but also provide you with valuable information that can be used to address their specific pain points.

Mastering the art of demonstrating empathy and understanding in a discovery sales meeting is essential for technology sales reps. By adopting a client-centric mindset, actively listening, and asking relevant questions, you can establish a strong rapport, build trust, and position yourself as a trusted advisor. By truly understanding the client's needs and goals, you can offer tailored solutions that meet their unique requirements and ultimately, drive successful sales outcomes.

Leveraging Pain Points to Present Solutions

It is during the discovery meeting that sales reps have the opportunity to truly understand their potential customers' pain points and challenges. By leveraging these pain points effectively, sales reps can present tailored solutions that address these specific needs. This chapter explores the art of leveraging pain points to present solutions, equipping technology sales reps with the skills they need to excel in their discovery sales meetings.

One of the first steps in leveraging pain points is actively listening to the customer. Sales reps must be attentive and empathetic, allowing the customer to express their challenges and concerns freely. By doing so, reps can gain valuable insights into the pain points that the customer is experiencing. This information serves as a foundation for delivering targeted solutions that directly address these pain points.

Once the pain points have been identified, it is essential for sales reps to showcase their understanding. This can be achieved by highlighting relevant case studies or success stories that demonstrate how similar pain points were resolved in the past. By illustrating their expertise and track record in solving similar challenges, sales reps can build trust with the customer and position themselves as a reliable source of solutions.

Next, sales reps should focus on presenting solutions that directly address the pain points. This requires a deep understanding of the product or service being offered, as well as the ability to articulate how the features and benefits align with the customer's specific needs. Sales reps should emphasize the tangible benefits that the customer will experience by implementing the proposed solution, such as increased efficiency, cost savings, or competitive advantage.

To further strengthen the sales pitch, sales reps can also leverage social proof. This involves showcasing testimonials or customer reviews that attest to the effectiveness of the proposed solution. By presenting real-world examples of how the solution has helped other customers overcome their pain points, sales reps can instill confidence in the customer and reinforce the value of their offerings.

Leveraging pain points to present solutions is a crucial skill for technology sales reps to master. By actively listening, showcasing understanding, and presenting tailored solutions, reps can effectively address the specific challenges faced by their customers. This subchapter provides valuable insights and strategies that can empower technology sales reps to excel in their discovery sales meetings and ultimately close more deals.

" It's easier to explain price once than to apologize for quality forever."

- ZIG ZIGLER

06

Presenting Solutions and Demonstrating Value

Tailoring Solutions to Customer Needs

One of the most crucial aspects of a successful discovery sales meeting is tailoring solutions to customer needs. It is not enough to have a great product or service; you must be able to effectively communicate its value to your potential customers. By understanding their unique challenges and requirements, you can position your offering as the perfect solution.

The first step in tailoring solutions to customer needs is thorough preparation. Before meeting with a prospect, it is essential to research their industry, competitors, and pain points. This information will help you identify potential areas where your product or service can make a significant impact. By demonstrating your understanding of their specific challenges, you will gain their trust and credibility.

During the discovery sales meeting, your goal should be to uncover the customer's needs and pain points. This can be achieved through active listening and asking open-ended questions. By allowing the customer to express their challenges and concerns, you can gain valuable insights into their unique situation. This information will serve as the foundation for tailoring your solution to meet their specific needs.

Once you have identified the customer's pain points, it is time to present your solution. However, it is essential to avoid a one-size-fits-all approach. Instead, customize your pitch to address the specific challenges and requirements discussed during the meeting. Highlight how your product or service can solve their problems and provide tangible benefits. Use case studies and success stories to illustrate how your solution has helped similar businesses in the past.

In addition to tailoring your solution to customer needs, it is crucial to be flexible and adaptable. As technology evolves rapidly, customer requirements may change. Stay up-to-date with the latest industry trends and adjust your offering accordingly. By continuously refining your solution, you can ensure that it remains relevant and valuable to your customers.

Tailoring solutions to customer needs is a critical skill for technology sales reps during a discovery sales meeting. Thorough preparation, active listening, and customization are key elements in this process. By understanding the customer's pain points and presenting a solution that addresses their specific challenges, you can establish yourself as a trusted advisor and increase your chances of closing the sale. Remember, technology is constantly evolving, so be prepared to adapt your offering to meet the changing needs of your customers.

Highlighting Key Features and Benefits

This chapter of "Mastering the Discovery Sales Meeting: A Guide for Technology Sales Reps" is specifically designed to provide invaluable insights and strategies for technology sales reps looking to excel in their discovery sales meetings.

The discovery sales meeting serves as an opportunity for technology sales reps to fully understand the needs, challenges, and goals of their potential clients. It is during this meeting that reps have the chance to highlight key features and benefits of their product or service, ultimately demonstrating how it can address the specific pain points of the client.

One of the key aspects of a successful discovery sales meeting is the ability to effectively highlight the unique features of the technology being sold. This chapter will delve into various techniques and approaches for showcasing these features in a way that resonates with the client. From creating compelling product demonstrations to utilizing case studies and testimonials, technology sales reps will learn how to present their product or service in the most compelling and persuasive manner.

Furthermore, this subchapter will emphasize the importance of focusing on the benefits that the technology can bring to the client's business. While features may be impressive, it is the benefits that truly convince clients to invest in a particular solution. By understanding the client's pain points and goals, technology sales reps can effectively articulate how their product can solve problems, increase efficiency, reduce costs, and improve overall business outcomes.

To truly master the art of highlighting key features and benefits, this chapter will also delve into the importance of active listening and asking the right questions during the discovery sales meeting. By actively listening to the client's responses and concerns, reps can tailor their approach, ensuring that the features and benefits they highlight are directly relevant and impactful to the client's specific needs.

By focusing on effective presentation techniques, emphasizing the benefits of the technology, and actively listening to the client, sales reps will be equipped with the tools they need to successfully close deals and build long-lasting client relationships.

Using Case Studies and Success Stories

The ability to effectively communicate the value of your products or services is crucial. One powerful tool to help you achieve this is the use of case studies and success stories during your discovery sales meetings. These tools provide real-life examples of how your offerings have positively impacted other companies, giving potential customers a tangible understanding of the benefits they can expect.

Case studies allow you to showcase your expertise by highlighting specific challenges your customers faced and how your solution helped overcome those hurdles. By presenting a well-crafted case study, you can demonstrate your understanding of your customers' pain points and illustrate how your product or service effectively addressed those issues. This not only instills confidence in your abilities but also helps potential customers envision the positive impact your offering can have on their own business.

Success stories, on the other hand, focus on the outcomes and benefits your customers have experienced after implementing your solution. By sharing these stories, you can paint a picture of the potential results and return on investment your prospects can expect. Success stories serve as powerful social proof, showcasing the positive experiences of others who have chosen your products or services. This can help alleviate any doubts or objections potential customers may have, making it easier to move them closer to a buying decision.

When utilizing case studies and success stories in your discovery sales meetings, it's important to keep a few key tips in mind. First, choose case studies and success stories that are relevant to your audience and their specific needs. Tailor your examples to address the pain points and challenges your prospects are likely facing, making it easier for them to see the value in your offering.

Second, focus on the results and outcomes achieved by your customers. Highlight the specific improvements in efficiency, cost savings, or revenue growth they experienced after implementing your solution. Quantifying these benefits with concrete numbers and statistics will enhance the credibility and impact of your case studies and success stories.

Lastly, be prepared to answer questions or address concerns that may arise from sharing these examples. While case studies and success stories are powerful tools, potential customers may have specific concerns or reservations that need to be addressed. Anticipate these objections and have well-thought-out responses ready to ensure you can effectively overcome any potential barriers to closing the sale.

Incorporating case studies and success stories into your discovery sales meetings is a proven strategy for technology sales reps. By leveraging real-life examples, you can effectively demonstrate the value and benefits your products or services can provide. Remember to choose relevant examples, focus on results, and be prepared to address any concerns that may arise. With these tools in your arsenal, you will be well-equipped to master the art of the discovery sales meeting and close more deals in the competitive technology sales industry.

Showing the ROI of Your Solution

One of the most crucial aspects of a successful discovery sales meeting is being able to demonstrate the return on investment (ROI) of your solution. As a technology sales rep, your primary goal is to convince potential customers that your product or service is not only valuable but also financially beneficial. This chapter will provide you with essential insights and strategies to effectively showcase the ROI of your solution during discovery sales meetings.

To begin with, it is important to thoroughly understand your customer's pain points and business objectives. By identifying their specific challenges and goals, you can tailor your solution to address their unique needs. Once you have a clear understanding of their requirements, you can then quantify the potential ROI your solution can bring to their organization.

When presenting the ROI, it is crucial to use concrete data and evidence. Utilize case studies, testimonials, and success stories from previous clients who have experienced a significant ROI after implementing your solution. This not only adds credibility to your claims but also helps potential customers envision the benefits they could achieve.

Furthermore, consider conducting a comprehensive cost-benefit analysis. Calculate the potential cost savings, increased productivity, and overall efficiency improvements that your solution can deliver. Break down the financial impact into tangible numbers, such as increased revenue, reduced operational expenses, or time saved. This will provide a clear and quantifiable picture of the ROI your solution can offer.

Another effective strategy is to offer a proof of concept or trial period. Allowing potential customers to test your solution firsthand in their own environment can be a powerful way to showcase its value. During this period, closely monitor and document any positive outcomes or improvements they experience. These real-time results can be shared with them, reinforcing the potential ROI and solidifying their confidence in your solution.

Finally, be prepared to address any objections or concerns regarding the ROI. Understand the potential risks or barriers that might prevent customers from fully embracing your solution. Anticipate their questions and provide compelling responses that highlight the long-term benefits and potential ROI they stand to gain.

Mastering the art of showing the ROI of your solution is essential for any technology sales rep. By effectively quantifying and demonstrating the financial benefits your solution can bring to potential customers, you will increase your chances of closing deals and building long-term relationships. Implement the strategies outlined in this chapter, and watch as your discovery sales meetings become more impactful and successful.

“ Remember that failure is an event, not a person. Yesterday ended last night.”

- ZIG ZIGLER

07

Handling Objections and Overcoming Resistance

Identifying Common Objections in the Discovery Sales Meeting

No matter how well you think your discovery sales meeting is going, it is not uncommon for sales reps to encounter objections during this stage.

Understanding and addressing objections effectively is key to moving the sales process forward and ultimately closing the deal. In this chapter, we will explore some of the most common objections that technology sales reps may encounter during the discovery sales meeting and provide strategies for overcoming them.

One common objection that may arise is budget constraints. Many potential customers may express concerns about the affordability of the technology solution being presented. To address this objection, sales reps can emphasize the value and return on investment that the solution can bring, highlighting cost-saving features and potential revenue growth opportunities.

Another objection that may arise is the fear of change. Some potential customers may be hesitant to adopt new technology due to concerns about disruption, integration challenges, or employee resistance. In response, sales reps can demonstrate the ease of implementation, provide case studies of successful transitions, and offer training and support resources to alleviate these fears.

Additionally, competition can be a significant objection in the technology sales space. Potential customers may express doubts about the uniqueness or superiority of the proposed solution compared to competitors. Sales reps can overcome this objection by showcasing the key differentiators and competitive advantages of their product or service, such as superior features, user-friendly interfaces, or exceptional customer support.

Lastly, objections related to risk and security are prevalent in the technology industry. Potential customers may express concerns about data breaches, system vulnerabilities, or the reliability of the solution. Sales reps can address these objections by providing robust security measures, certifications, and testimonials from satisfied customers who have experienced no issues with the technology.

By proactively identifying and addressing these common objections, technology sales reps can enhance their discovery sales meetings and increase their chances of closing the deal. The key is to understand the objections as opportunities for clarification and education, rather than roadblocks. With the right strategies and a deep understanding of their potential customers' needs, technology sales reps can successfully navigate objections and move closer to achieving their sales goals.

Responding to Objections with Confidence

In sales, objections are bound to arise during the discovery sales meeting. Whether it's concerns about budget, competition, or the suitability of your solution, objections can often be seen as obstacles standing in the way of closing the deal. However, with the right mindset and approach, objections can actually be opportunities to showcase your expertise and build trust with your potential clients.

To respond to objections with confidence, it's crucial to be well-prepared and knowledgeable about your product or service. Take the time to thoroughly understand your solution's features, benefits, and unique selling points. This will allow you to address objections with clarity and conviction, showcasing your expertise and instilling confidence in your potential clients.

When facing objections, it's essential to actively listen and understand the concerns being raised. Rather than immediately countering objections with a pre-rehearsed response, take the time to empathize and validate the client's concerns. By demonstrating that you genuinely understand their perspective, you can establish rapport and foster a more collaborative environment.

Once you have a clear understanding of the objection, it's time to respond effectively. Begin by acknowledging the objection and its validity. This shows that you respect the client's viewpoint and are not dismissive of their concerns. Next, provide a well-thought-out response that directly addresses the objection and offers a solution. Be concise, factual, and avoid making promises you cannot keep. Your response should be tailored to the client's specific situation and clearly demonstrate how your solution can overcome their objections.

To respond to objections with confidence, it's also crucial to remain calm and composed throughout the conversation. Objections can sometimes feel like personal attacks, but it's important to remember that they are not. Rather than becoming defensive or argumentative, maintain a professional demeanor and keep the focus on finding a solution that meets the client's needs.

Finally, when responding to objections, always be prepared to move on to next steps. After addressing the objection, reaffirm the value and benefits of your solution. Emphasize how it aligns with the client's goals and objectives, and ask for their commitment to move forward. By doing so, you can demonstrate your confidence in your offering and inspire confidence in your potential clients.

Responding to objections with confidence is a crucial skill for technology sales reps during the discovery sales meeting. By being well-prepared, actively listening, empathizing, and providing well-thought-out responses, you can turn objections into opportunities to showcase your expertise and build trust with your potential clients. Remember to remain calm, professional, and always ask to move on to next steps. With these strategies in place, you'll be well-equipped to handle objections and close deals successfully.

Addressing Price Concerns

One of the most common concerns that arises during a discovery sales meeting is price. As a technology sales rep, it is crucial to address these concerns effectively in order to build trust with potential clients and close deals successfully. This chapter will provide you with valuable insights and strategies to handle price concerns and navigate through the discovery sales meeting.

1. Understand the Client's Perspective: The first step in addressing price concerns is to understand the client's perspective. Put yourself in their shoes and try to comprehend their budget constraints, priorities, and expectations. By doing so, you can tailor your approach accordingly and offer solutions that align with their needs.

2. Emphasize the Value: Instead of focusing solely on the price, shift the conversation towards the value that your technology solution provides. Highlight the benefits, return on investment, and long-term cost savings that the client can expect. This will help them see the bigger picture and understand the value proposition of your product or service.

3. Offer Flexible Pricing Options: Every client has different financial circumstances, so it is essential to offer flexible pricing options. This could include tiered pricing plans, monthly subscriptions, or customized packages that suit their specific requirements. By providing options, you demonstrate your willingness to work with the client and accommodate their financial limitations.

4. Provide Evidence of ROI: Numbers speak louder than words. Back up your claims with real data and evidence of the return on investment (ROI) that your previous clients have experienced. Case studies, testimonials, and success stories can be powerful tools to convince potential clients that your technology solution is worth the investment.

5. Address Competitors' Pricing: In the competitive landscape of technology sales, it is crucial to address competitors' pricing tactfully. Highlight the unique features, superior quality, and added value that your solution offers compared to your

competitors. By focusing on what sets you apart, you can justify a higher price point and position your product or service as the best choice.

Remember, price concerns are a natural part of the sales process. By addressing them proactively, understanding the client's perspective, emphasizing value, offering flexible pricing options, providing evidence of ROI, and addressing competitors' pricing, you can effectively navigate through price concerns and increase your chances of closing successful deals in the discovery sales meeting.

Overcoming Resistance and Gaining Buy-in

A critical step in the sales process is building relationships and ultimately closing deals. However, even the most skilled reps may encounter resistance from potential clients during this crucial stage. Overcoming resistance and gaining buy-in from prospects requires a strategic approach that combines effective communication, persuasive techniques, and a deep understanding of the client's needs and pain points.

One of the first steps in overcoming resistance is to establish rapport and trust with the prospect. Reps should aim to build a genuine connection by actively listening to the client's concerns and demonstrating empathy. By showing that you understand their challenges and have their best interests at heart, you can create a foundation of trust that will facilitate the rest of the sales process.

Another key aspect of overcoming resistance is effectively addressing objections. Prospects may have doubts or hesitations about investing in new technology, and it is the sales rep's responsibility to address these concerns head-on. Rather than dismissing objections, sales reps should view them as opportunities to demonstrate their expertise and provide valuable insights. By providing compelling evidence, case studies, and testimonials, sales reps can alleviate concerns and build confidence in the prospect's mind.

Additionally, gaining buy-in requires a thorough understanding of the prospect's needs and pain points. Technology sales reps should conduct extensive research and preparation before the discovery sales meeting to identify the specific challenges the client is facing. By tailoring the conversation to address these pain points and offering personalized solutions, sales reps can demonstrate their value and relevance, increasing the likelihood of buy-in.

Furthermore, leveraging the power of storytelling can be a persuasive tool in gaining buy-in. By sharing success stories and illustrating how your technology solutions have helped similar clients overcome challenges and achieve their goals, you can paint a vivid picture of the potential benefits. Stories have a unique ability to engage emotions and create a sense of urgency, compelling prospects to take action.

Overcoming resistance and gaining buy-in in the discovery sales meeting requires a combination of effective communication, addressing objections, understanding client needs, and utilizing the power of storytelling. By mastering these techniques, technology sales reps can build trust, alleviate concerns, and ultimately close deals successfully.

" Lack of direction, not lack of time, is the problem. We all have 24-hour days."

- ZIG ZIGLER

08

Closing the Discovery Sales Meeting

Summarizing Customer Needs and Pain Points

It is during the discovery meeting that sales reps have the opportunity to truly understand their customers' needs and pain points. By effectively summarizing these key aspects, sales reps can lay the foundation for a successful sales pitch and ultimately close the deal.

Understanding customer needs is the first step in the discovery sales meeting. It involves asking the right questions and actively listening to the customer's responses. By doing so, sales reps can gain valuable insights into what the customer is looking for in a technology solution. This could include specific features, functionality, or even integration capabilities. By summarizing these needs, sales reps can demonstrate their understanding of the customer's requirements and establish trust.

Equally important is identifying and addressing the customer's pain points. Pain points are the challenges or frustrations that customers are experiencing and are seeking to solve. By delving deeper into these pain points, sales reps can position their technology solution as the answer to the customer's problems. Summarizing these pain points not only shows empathy but also allows sales reps to tailor their pitch to address these specific issues, making their solution more compelling and relevant to the customer.

The key to effective summarization lies in clarity and conciseness. Sales reps should avoid overwhelming the customer with excessive information or technical jargon. Instead, they should focus on distilling the customer's needs and pain points into concise and easily understandable summaries. This allows the customer to see that the sales rep truly understands their situation and has the expertise to deliver the right solution.

Summarizing customer needs and pain points also serves as a reference point throughout the sales process. It helps sales reps stay focused on the customer's requirements and ensures that their pitch remains aligned with the customer's priorities. By regularly revisiting these summaries, sales reps can reinforce their understanding of the customer's needs and pain points, making them better equipped to address any objections or concerns that may arise.

Mastering the art of summarizing customer needs and pain points is essential for technology sales reps during the discovery sales meeting. By effectively summarizing these key aspects, sales reps can demonstrate their understanding of the customer's requirements, position their solution as the answer to the customer's problems, and ultimately increase their chances of closing the deal.

Presenting a Compelling Solution

This chapter focuses on the significant aspect of presenting a compelling solution, which is the key to winning over potential clients and gaining their trust. During a discovery sales meeting, sales reps have the opportunity to showcase their expertise and demonstrate how their products or services can solve the client's pain points and meet their specific needs. The goal is to present a solution that not only addresses the client's challenges but also delivers tangible benefits and a clear return on investment.

To present a compelling solution, it is essential for sales reps to thoroughly understand the client's requirements and pain points. This involves active listening and asking the right questions to gain a deep understanding of the client's business objectives, challenges, and desired outcomes. Armed with this knowledge, sales reps can tailor their solution to align perfectly with the client's needs, making it more convincing and compelling.

A compelling solution presentation should be structured, clear, and concise. It should highlight the unique value proposition of the product or service and emphasize how it can address the client's pain points. Visual aids, such as charts, graphs, or case studies, can be used to support the presentation and provide evidence of the solution's effectiveness.

Additionally, sales reps should focus on articulating the benefits and outcomes that the client can expect from implementing the solution. This could include increased efficiency, cost savings, improved productivity, or competitive advantage. By demonstrating the value that the solution brings to the table, sales reps can build credibility and create a sense of urgency for the client to take action.

Furthermore, it is crucial for sales reps to address any potential objections or concerns that the client may have during the presentation. By proactively anticipating and addressing these objections, sales reps can instill confidence in the client and alleviate any doubts they may have.

Presenting a compelling solution is a crucial component of the discovery sales meeting for technology sales reps. By thoroughly understanding the client's needs, tailoring the solution to meet those needs, and effectively articulating the value and benefits, reps can increase their chances of closing deals and achieving success in the competitive technology sales landscape.

Addressing Any Remaining Concerns

Even after a successful discovery sales meeting, there might be lingering concerns or doubts that need to be addressed. This section aims to guide technology sales reps on how to address any remaining concerns and ensure a smooth transition from the discovery phase to closing the deal. One of the first steps in addressing any remaining concerns is active listening. During the discovery sales meeting, sales reps must have paid close attention to the client's pain points, challenges, and requirements. By actively listening and taking note of these concerns, reps can demonstrate their attentiveness and empathy towards the client's unique situation. This not only builds trust but also helps reps in framing their responses to address those concerns effectively.

Next, sales reps should be prepared with relevant information and evidence to support their claims. Clients may have doubts about the effectiveness or reliability of a specific solution. Sales reps must be equipped with case studies, testimonials, and success stories that demonstrate how their product or service has helped similar clients in the past. Providing tangible evidence will help address any lingering concerns and provide reassurance to potential clients.

Additionally, it is crucial to maintain open lines of communication throughout the sales process. Clients may have questions or concerns that arise after the discovery meeting. Sales reps should be readily available to address these concerns promptly. By being responsive and proactive in addressing any new concerns, sales reps can ensure that clients feel heard and supported.

Furthermore, reps should consider offering a trial or pilot program to potential clients. This allows clients to experience the solution firsthand, alleviating any doubts about its efficacy. By offering a risk-free opportunity to test the technology, reps can help clients overcome any remaining concerns and make a more informed decision.

Addressing any remaining concerns is a crucial step in the discovery sales process. Active listening, providing relevant evidence, maintaining open lines of communication, and offering trial programs are effective strategies for technology sales reps to address and alleviate any doubts or concerns that potential clients may have. By implementing these strategies, reps can increase their chances of successfully closing deals and building long-lasting partnerships with clients.

Securing Next Steps and Follow-up

The true success of a discovery sales meeting lies not only in the initial conversation but also in the steps taken afterward to secure next steps and ensure a fruitful follow-up.

Securing next steps is crucial to maintaining momentum and keeping the sales process moving forward. It involves setting clear expectations and establishing a roadmap for the next phase. As a technology sales rep, your goal is to guide your prospects through the sales funnel while building trust and credibility. This subchapter will equip you with the necessary strategies to secure next steps effectively.

To begin, it is essential to recap the key takeaways and mutually agreed-upon action items at the end of the discovery sales meeting. Summarize the prospect's pain points, objectives, and the proposed solution you discussed. This serves as a foundation for future discussions and ensures that everyone is on the same page.

Next, discuss the specific next steps with your prospect. Identify the key milestones, such as scheduling a demo, conducting a technical assessment, or arranging a meeting with key decision-makers. Clearly communicate the purpose, timeline, and expected outcomes of each step. This level of transparency builds trust and demonstrates your commitment to their success.

Follow-up plays a pivotal role in securing next steps. After the discovery sales meeting, promptly send a personalized follow-up email that highlights the discussed points and reiterates the agreed-upon next steps. This reinforces your professionalism and keeps the conversation fresh in their minds.

Additionally, leverage technology to automate and streamline the follow-up process. Utilize customer relationship management (CRM) tools to send reminders, schedule calls or meetings, and track progress. This not only saves time but also ensures that no steps are overlooked or forgotten.

Finally, always be proactive in your follow-up efforts. If a prospect fails to respond or misses a scheduled call, it is your responsibility to reach out and re-engage them. Show persistence without being pushy, as building relationships often requires multiple touchpoints.

By mastering the art of securing next steps and following up effectively, technology sales reps can significantly enhance their chances of closing deals and nurturing long-term customer relationships. Remember, the discovery sales meeting is just the beginning, and it is the subsequent steps that truly solidify the foundation for success.

" If people like you, they'll listen to you, but if they trust you, they'll do business with you."

- ZIG ZIGLER

09

Maximizing Post-Meeting Opportunities

Evaluating the Success of the Discovery Sales Meeting

The discovery sales meeting holds immense importance. It serves as a crucial opportunity for sales reps to gather valuable insights about their potential customers' needs, pain points, and goals. However, the true measure of success lies not only in conducting these meetings but also in evaluating their effectiveness. In this chapter, we will explore various strategies and techniques to assess the success of your discovery sales meetings and enhance your overall sales performance.

The first step in evaluating the success of your discovery sales meeting is to define clear objectives. What do you aim to achieve during these interactions? Is it gathering information about the prospect's requirements, understanding their decision-making process, or building rapport? By setting specific goals, you can gauge whether you were able to accomplish them by the end of the meeting.

Another vital aspect of evaluation is the identification of key performance indicators (KPIs). These metrics will help you track your progress and measure the effectiveness of your discovery sales meetings. KPIs could include the number of new insights gained, the quality of questions asked, or the ratio of closed deals from prospects who attended these meetings. By analyzing these KPIs, you can identify areas of improvement and adapt your sales approach accordingly.

Feedback from both sides of the table is invaluable when evaluating the success of a discovery sales meeting. After each meeting, solicit feedback from your potential customer to gain insights into their perception of the meeting's value. Did they feel their needs were understood? Did they believe the meeting was a productive use of their time? This feedback can help you refine your approach and tailor future meetings to better meet the needs of your prospects.

Additionally, seeking feedback from your sales team or manager can provide valuable insights. They can offer an objective perspective on your performance, highlight areas of improvement, and provide guidance on how to enhance the effectiveness of your discovery sales meetings.

To further evaluate the success of your discovery sales meetings, consider implementing post-meeting analysis. Review your notes, identify any missed opportunities or areas that require further exploration, and develop action plans to address them in subsequent meetings. This analysis will not only help you improve your sales techniques but also demonstrate your commitment to continuous improvement to potential customers.

Evaluating the success of your discovery sales meetings is essential for technology sales reps. By defining clear objectives, identifying KPIs, seeking feedback from prospects and colleagues, and conducting post-meeting analysis, you can continuously refine your approach and enhance the effectiveness of your discovery sales meetings. Remember, the ultimate goal is not just to conduct these meetings but to extract maximum value from them, leading to increased sales and customer satisfaction.

Leveraging Post-Meeting Feedback for Improvement

The success of a discovery meeting does not solely depend on the preparation and execution during the meeting. It also requires diligent post-meeting follow-up and leveraging feedback for continuous improvement.

Post-meeting feedback is a powerful tool that can help technology sales reps fine-tune their approach, identify areas of improvement, and ultimately increase their chances of closing deals. By actively seeking feedback from both the customer and internal stakeholders

One way to leverage post-meeting feedback is by conducting a thorough self-assessment. This involves reflecting on your own performance during the meeting and identifying areas where you excelled and areas where you could have done better. Did you effectively communicate the value proposition of your product or service? Did you ask the right questions to uncover the customer's pain points? Analyzing your own performance will help you identify areas for personal growth and skill development.

Additionally, soliciting feedback from the customer can provide invaluable insights. Reach out to your customers after the meeting and ask for their thoughts on the interaction. Were they satisfied with the information provided? Were their concerns adequately addressed? This feedback can help you understand the customer's perspective and identify any gaps in your approach.

Internal feedback is equally important. Collaborate with your team members or sales manager to discuss the meeting and gather their observations. They may have valuable insights that you may have missed or suggestions on how to improve your sales pitch. This collaborative approach fosters a culture of continuous learning and improvement within the sales team.

Once you have collected feedback from various sources, it is essential to take action. Create an action plan based on the feedback received and implement changes in your approach for future meetings. Remember, the goal is not to be perfect but to consistently improve and deliver a better customer experience.

Leveraging post-meeting feedback is a critical step in mastering the discovery sales meeting. By conducting a self-assessment, seeking feedback from customers and internal stakeholders, and taking action based on the insights gained, technology sales reps can continuously improve their skills and increase their chances of success. Embrace feedback as a valuable tool for growth, and you will see remarkable progress in your sales career.

Nurturing Relationships with Prospects

During a discovery meeting, sales reps have the opportunity to not only understand the needs and pain points of their prospects but also to establish a strong and lasting relationship.

Building relationships with prospects is essential for success in the competitive technology industry. It is not enough to simply make a pitch and hope for the best. Technology sales reps must invest time and effort into nurturing these relationships, as they can often be the differentiating factor between closing a deal or losing it to a competitor.

One of the key aspects of nurturing relationships with prospects is active listening. During the discovery sales meeting, it is essential for sales reps to listen attentively to their prospects, not only to understand their challenges but also to show genuine interest. By actively listening and asking relevant follow-up questions, sales reps can demonstrate their understanding and build trust with prospects.

Another important element in nurturing relationships with prospects is providing value. Technology sales reps should focus on offering insights, guidance, and solutions that are tailored to their prospects' specific needs. By positioning themselves as trusted advisors rather than pushy salespeople, reps can establish credibility and foster a stronger connection with their prospects.

Additionally, maintaining consistent and timely communication is crucial. Following up promptly after the discovery sales meeting shows prospects that their business is valued and that the sales rep is committed to their success. Regular check-ins, whether through phone calls, emails, or social media, can help to keep the relationship alive and demonstrate ongoing support.

Lastly, technology sales reps must always strive to exceed expectations. Going above and beyond what is expected can leave a lasting impression on prospects. Whether it is by providing additional resources, offering personalized demos, or connecting them with industry experts, sales reps can showcase their commitment to helping their prospects achieve their goals.

Nurturing relationships with prospects is a vital aspect of the discovery sales meeting for technology sales reps. By actively listening, providing value, maintaining consistent communication, and exceeding expectations, reps can establish strong and lasting connections with prospects. These relationships not only increase the likelihood of closing deals but also pave the way for long-term success in the technology sales industry.

Expanding Opportunities for Future Sales

This chapter will explore strategies to expand opportunities for future sales during these meetings, providing valuable insights for technology sales reps.

One key aspect of the discovery sales meeting is understanding the customer's needs and pain points. By actively listening and asking insightful questions, sales reps can gain a deep understanding of the challenges faced by the client. This knowledge forms the foundation for identifying opportunities to provide tailored solutions that meet their specific requirements.

To expand opportunities for future sales, sales reps should focus on showcasing the value of their products or services. By effectively articulating how their offerings can address the client's pain points and deliver tangible benefits, reps can position themselves as trusted advisors. This builds credibility and increases the likelihood of future sales opportunities.

Furthermore, reps should actively seek to uncover additional needs and opportunities during the discovery sales meeting. By probing deeper into the client's business processes and goals, reps can identify areas where their products or services can provide further value. This could involve upselling or cross-selling complementary solutions, ultimately expanding the scope of the sales opportunity.

Building strong relationships is another vital component of expanding future sales opportunities. By demonstrating a genuine interest in the client's success and investing time in cultivating a relationship, technology sales reps can create a strong foundation for ongoing sales engagement. This may involve regular check-ins, providing relevant industry insights, or offering post-sales support to ensure customer satisfaction.

Lastly, sales reps should utilize the discovery sales meeting as a platform for gathering valuable feedback. By actively seeking feedback on their products or services, reps can identify areas for improvement and innovation. This customer-centric approach not only enhances the overall customer experience but also opens doors for future sales through product enhancements and updates.

The discovery sales meeting is an essential opportunity for technology sales reps to expand future sales. By understanding customer needs, showcasing value, identifying additional opportunities, building relationships, and gathering feedback, reps can position themselves as trusted advisors and maximize their sales potential. Implementing these strategies will enable technology sales reps to effectively navigate discovery sales meetings and unlock new avenues for success in the ever-evolving technology sales landscape.

" If you are not willing to learn, no one can help you. If you are determined to learn, no one can stop you."

- ZIG ZIGLER

10

Conclusion

Recap of Key Concepts

In this chapter, we will take a moment to recap the key concepts covered in this book, "Mastering the Discovery Sales Meeting: A Guide for Technology Sales Reps." As technology sales reps, mastering the art of the discovery sales meeting is crucial for success in our field. So, let's review the fundamental concepts we have explored throughout this book.

Firstly, we emphasized the importance of thorough preparation before any discovery sales meeting. This includes researching the prospect, their industry, pain points, and any potential solutions that our technology can provide. By doing so, we can tailor our approach and deliver a more targeted and impactful meeting.

Next, we discussed the significance of setting clear objectives for every discovery sales meeting. These objectives should align with the prospect's needs, allowing us to understand their challenges, goals, and expectations. By setting these objectives, we can keep the conversation on track and ensure that we provide relevant solutions.

Furthermore, we discussed the importance of presenting our technology solutions in a compelling manner. By focusing on the prospect's pain points and demonstrating how our product or service can address those pain points, we can showcase the value and benefits of our offering. We also highlighted the significance of storytelling and using case studies to provide real-life examples of how our technology has positively impacted similar businesses.

Lastly, we stressed the importance of follow-up and maintaining strong relationships with prospects. By promptly addressing any questions or concerns, we can demonstrate our commitment to their success. Additionally, staying in touch and providing valuable insights even after the sale can help foster long-term partnerships and generate referrals.

In conclusion, mastering the discovery sales meeting is a critical skill for technology sales reps. By thoroughly preparing, setting clear objectives, asking effective questions, actively listening, presenting solutions, and maintaining strong relationships, we can enhance our success in this field. Remember, every interaction with a prospect is an opportunity to provide value and make a lasting impression.

Final Thoughts on Mastering the Discovery Sales Meeting

Congratulations! You have reached the end of this guide, and by now, you should have a solid understanding of how to master the discovery sales meeting as a technology sales rep. The discovery sales meeting is a crucial step in the sales process, as it sets the foundation for a successful partnership with your clients. In this final subchapter, we will summarize the key points covered throughout this book and leave you with some final thoughts to keep in mind as you continue to refine your skills in conducting discovery sales meetings.

First and foremost, remember that preparation is key. Before every discovery sales meeting, take the time to research your prospect's industry, competitors, and challenges they may be facing. This will enable you to ask insightful questions that demonstrate your expertise and show your prospect that you understand their unique needs.

During the meeting, active listening is essential. Truly understand your prospect's pain points, goals, and objectives. Ask open-ended questions that encourage them to elaborate and provide you with valuable information. Remember, the discovery sales meeting is not about pitching your product or service but rather about understanding your prospect's needs and aligning your solution accordingly.

In order to build trust and rapport, make sure to establish a genuine connection with your prospect. Show empathy, be authentic, and demonstrate that you genuinely care about helping them solve their challenges. This will not only make the discovery sales meeting more enjoyable for both parties but will also increase the likelihood of a successful partnership in the future.

Lastly, always follow up after the discovery sales meeting. Send a personalized email thanking your prospect for their time and reiterate the key points discussed during the meeting. This will not only show your professionalism but will also keep the conversation going and demonstrate your commitment to their success.

As a technology sales rep, mastering the discovery sales meeting is a continuous learning process. Each meeting will present new challenges and opportunities to improve. By implementing the strategies and techniques discussed in this book, you will be well-equipped to navigate these meetings with confidence and close more deals.

Remember, the discovery sales meeting is your chance to shine and differentiate yourself from the competition. Embrace the opportunity to truly understand your prospect's needs, build trust, and position yourself as a trusted advisor. With practice and dedication, you will become a master of the discovery sales meeting and achieve greater success in your technology sales career.